MIME
VERY OWN
BOOK

Published 2011 by Medallion Press, Inc.

The MEDALLION PRESS LOGO
is a registered trademark of Medallion Press, Inc.

ISBN# 978-1605422-55-8

10 9 8 7 6 5 4 3 2 1
First Edition

DEDICATION

To God Himself. I'm sorry I argued with You about the tall, skinny thing. Seems You knew what You were doing after all.

—Doug

To Rain. I hope this book gives you as many repeat laughs as your face gives me repeat smiles.

—SAP

To Sara, Magpie, and Gabriel. My heart loves your heart.
—Adam

This book is dedicated to my mother . . . and DEFINITELY NOT to my dad.
—Eric

doug jones . eric curtis . scott allen perry . adam mock

MIME
VERY OWN
BOOK

MEDALLION
PRESS

Foreword

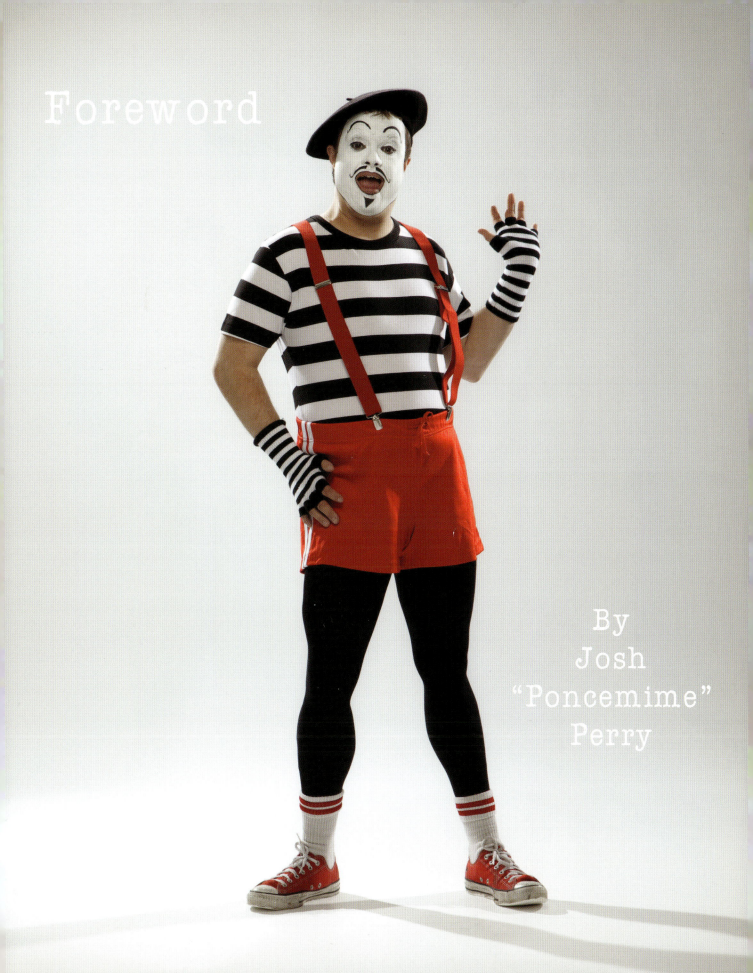

By
Josh
"Poncemime"
Perry

I love my
Dougie.

He makes me laugh.

He is the nicest guy
on the planet.

I love his
movies.

I love
Doug Jones.

He calls me
his Precious,
and I love that
a lot.

It makes
me happy.

Dougie was a
great zombie . . .

. . . and Pan
and
Pale Man.

. . . and Abe Sapien
from *Hellboy* and
Hellboy II.

And I loved it
when he was
the
Silver
Surfer . . .

He works so
hard to make
all his movies.
I love his
work, and
maybe someday
me and Doug
should be
in a movie
together

That would be fun.

He should play a giant,
and I could be
his little
man.

I love my
Dougie
so much,
that ras...

. . . and one and only,
my man Doug . . .

. . . that no-good homeboy,
that rascal,
that precious . . .

I love you, Dougie.
You're the best there is forever and ever, man.

XXXoooXXX,
Josh
"The Poncemime"
Perry

Unspoken

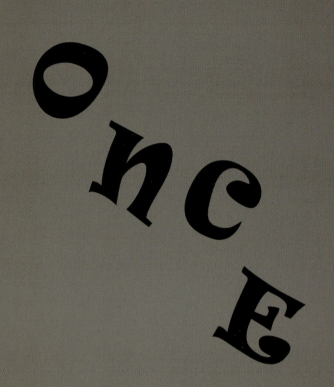

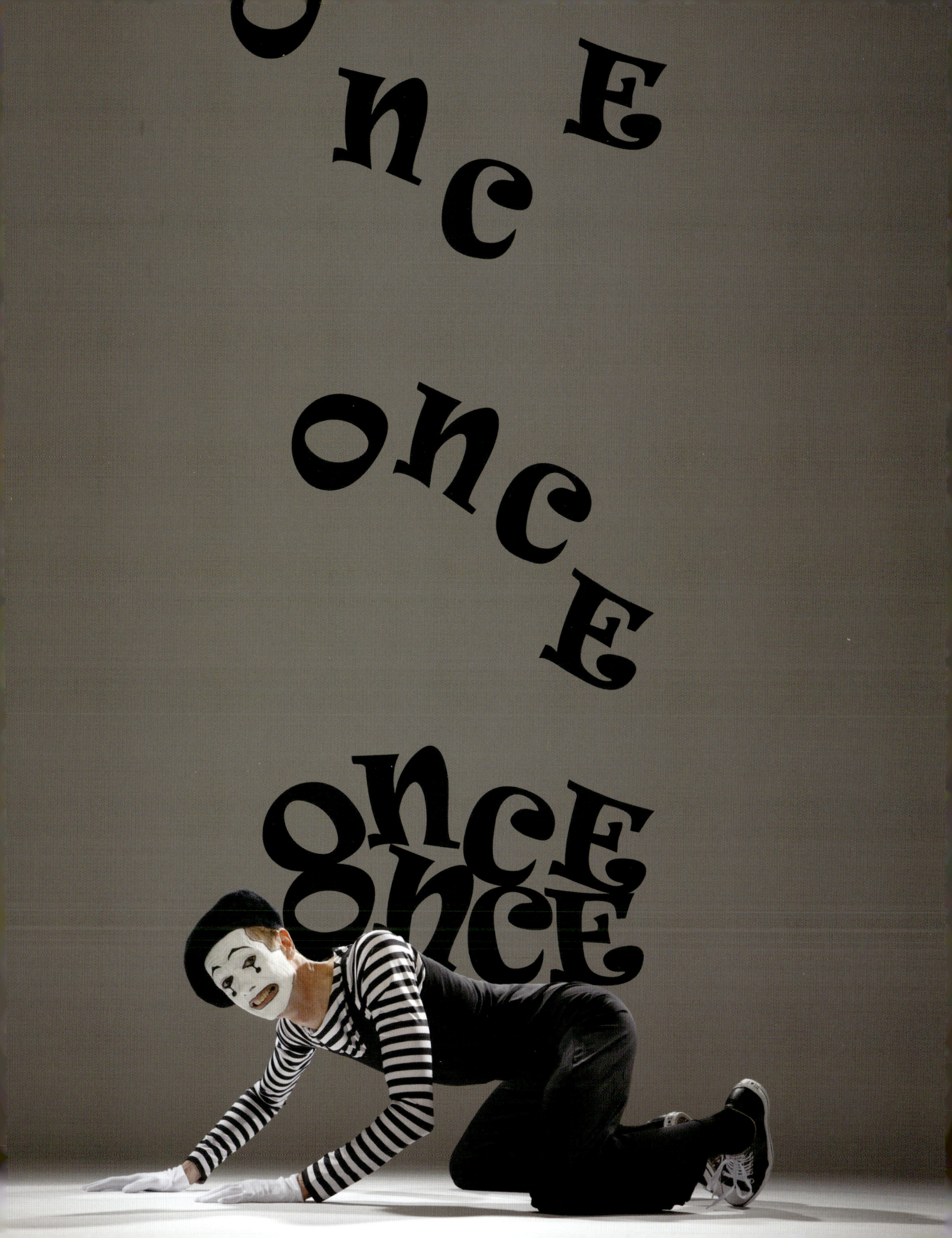
once
once
once
once

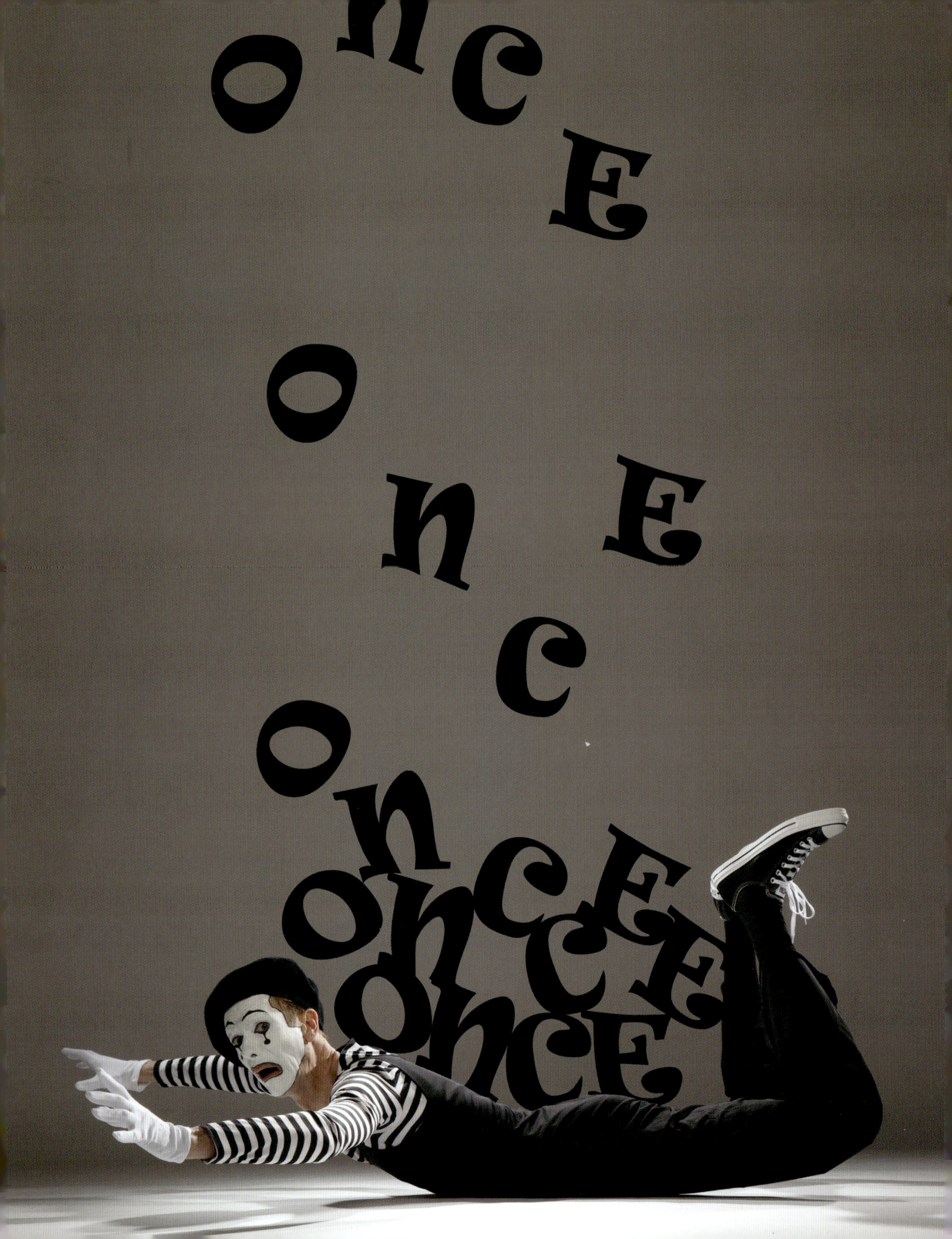

Timeless . . . not mimeless

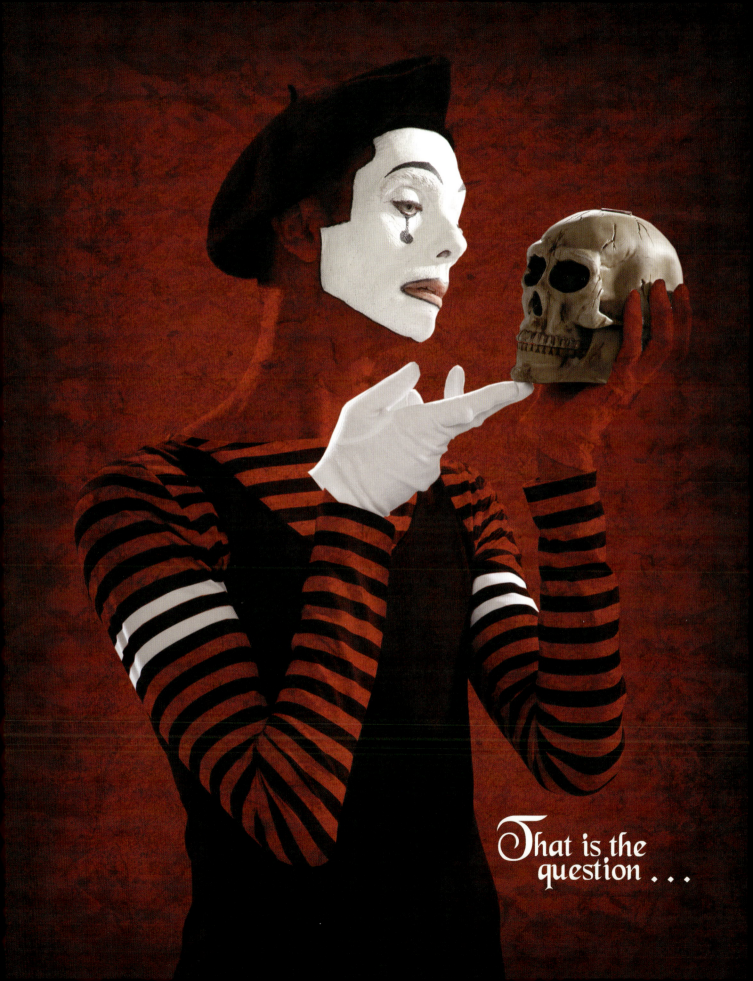

That is the
question . . .

Mime your manners

Mime a se
Mime a sa
Mime ma coo sa

Doug Jones
Thriller

DOUG JONE

BAD

Cinema & Television

MSI:
MIME SCENE INVESTIGATION

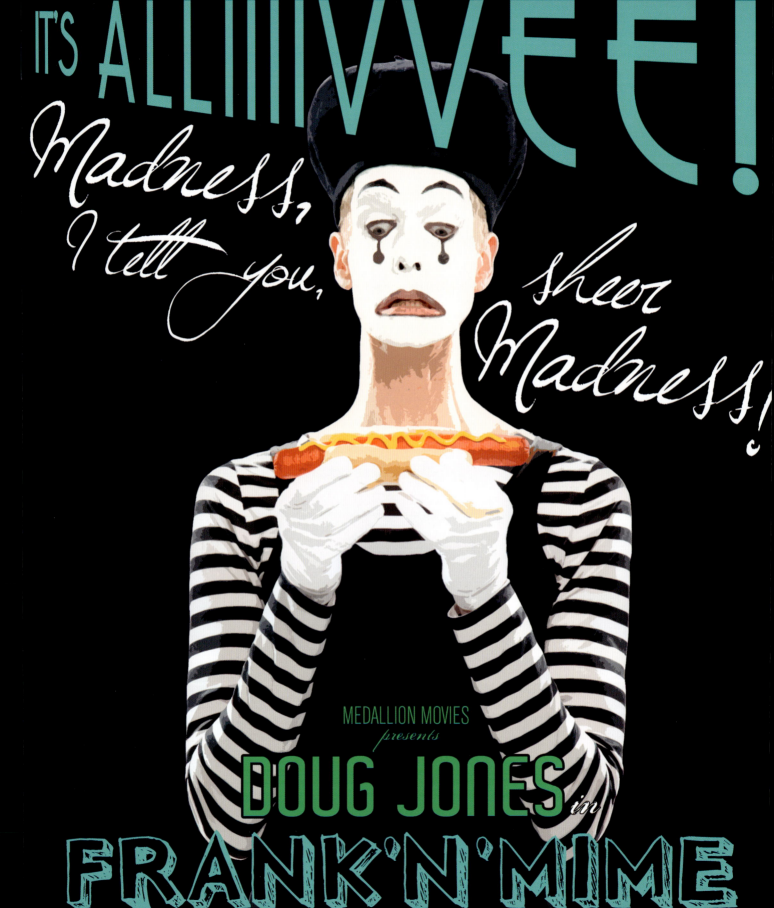

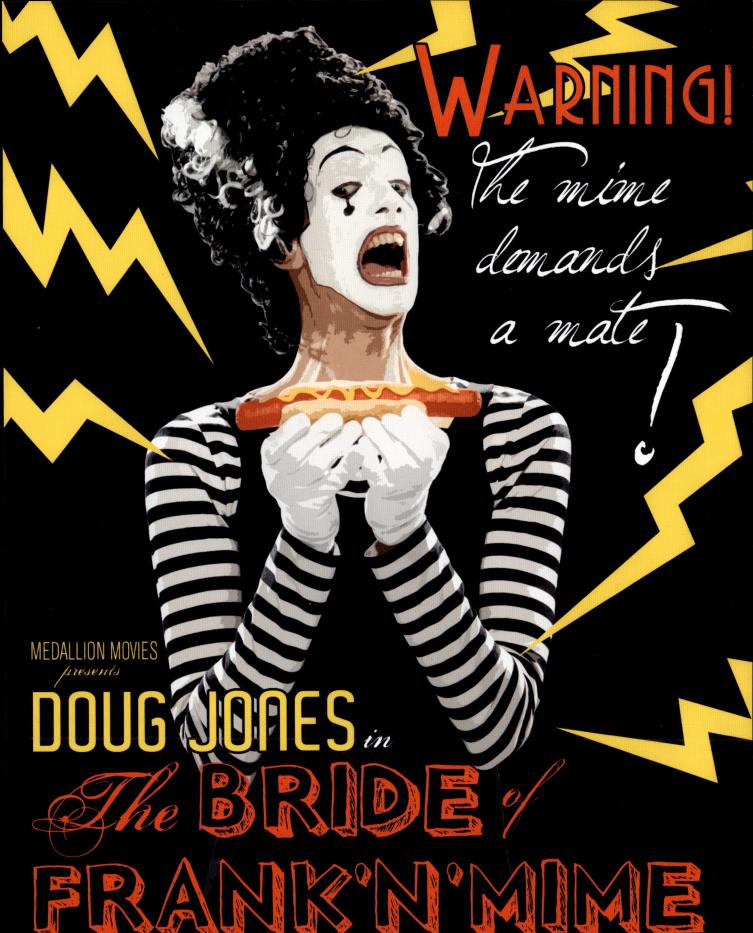

STARRING
DOUG JONES AS JACK TORRANCE & WENDY TORRANCE

THE MIMING

don't say anything

DOUG JONES

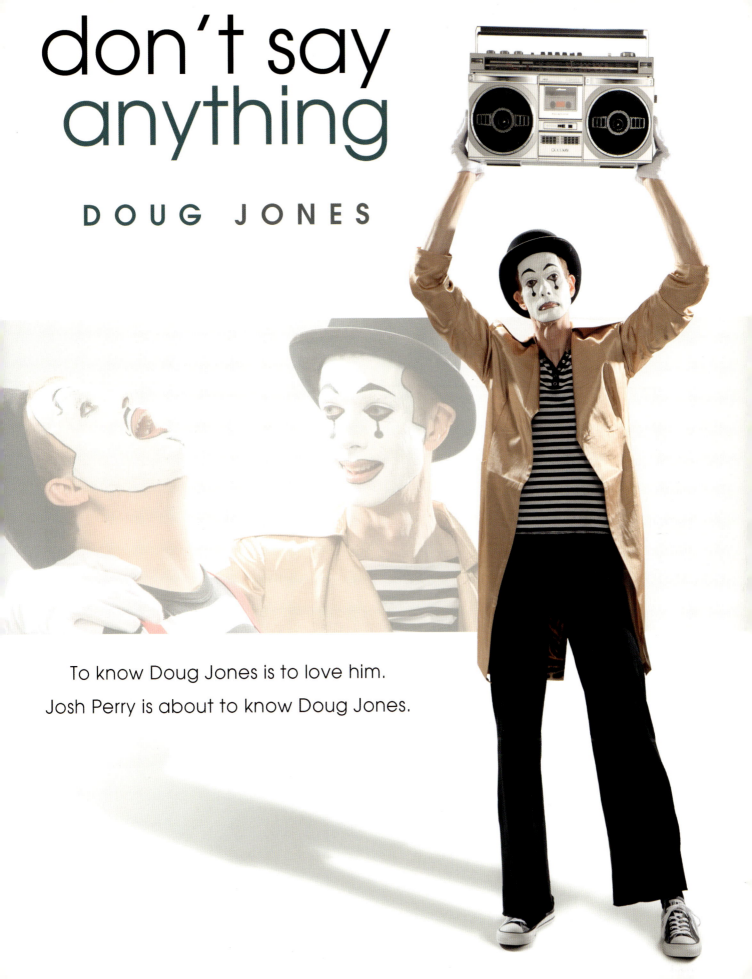

To know Doug Jones is to love him.

Josh Perry is about to know Doug Jones.

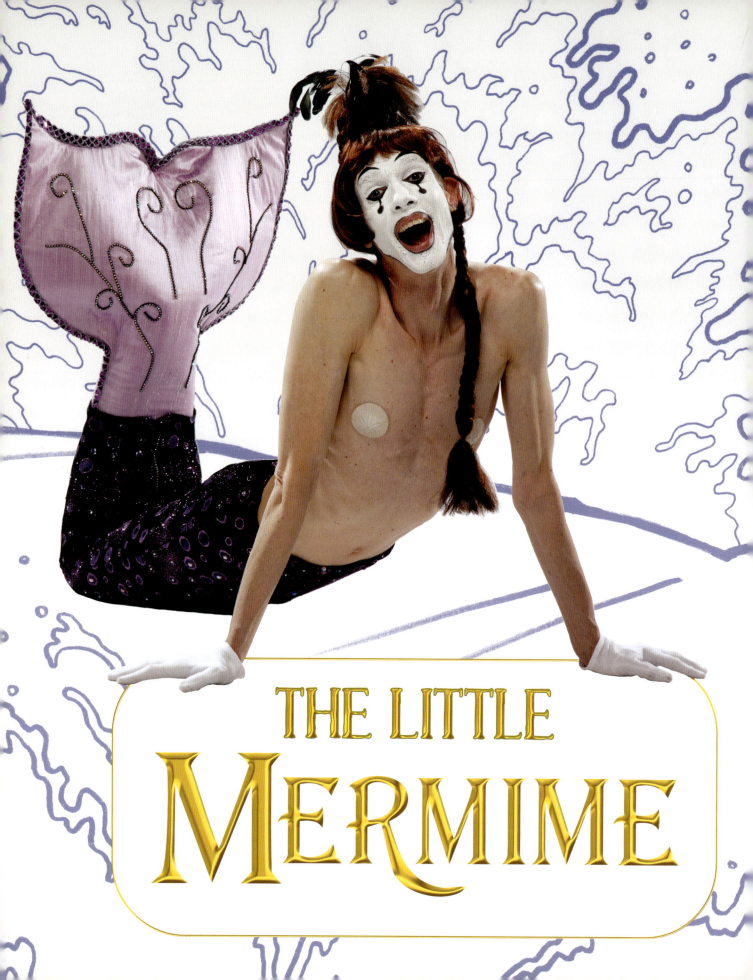

THE LITTLE
MERMIME

Romance

Horror

Zombies

Rise of the Zombies

Suspense

Comedy

Once upon a mime

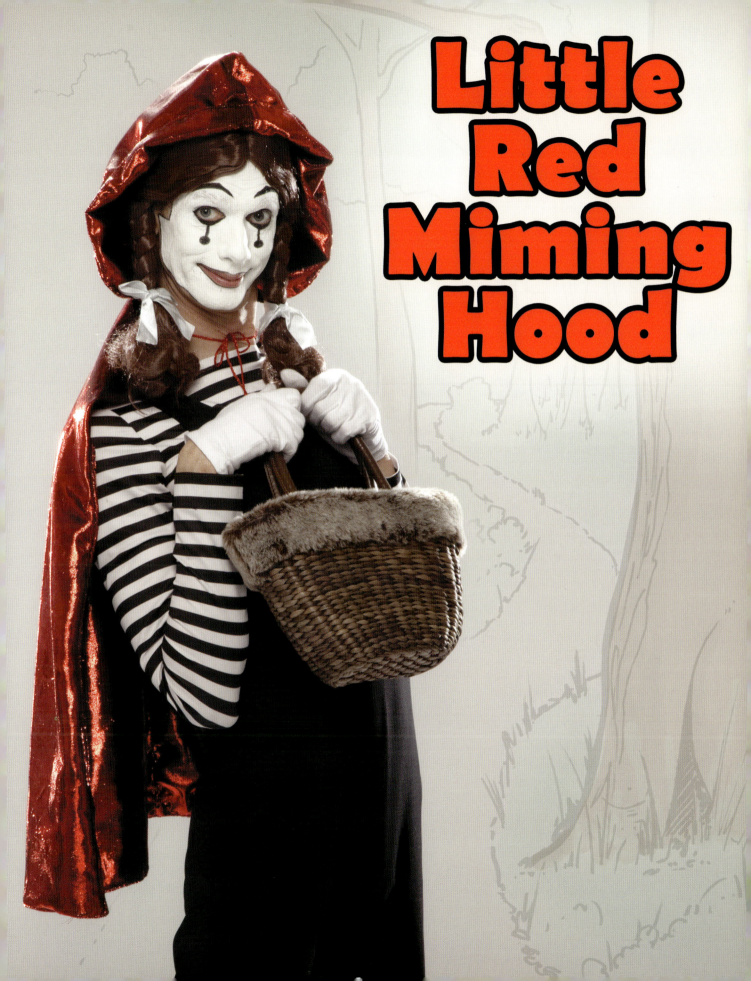

Little Red Miming Hood

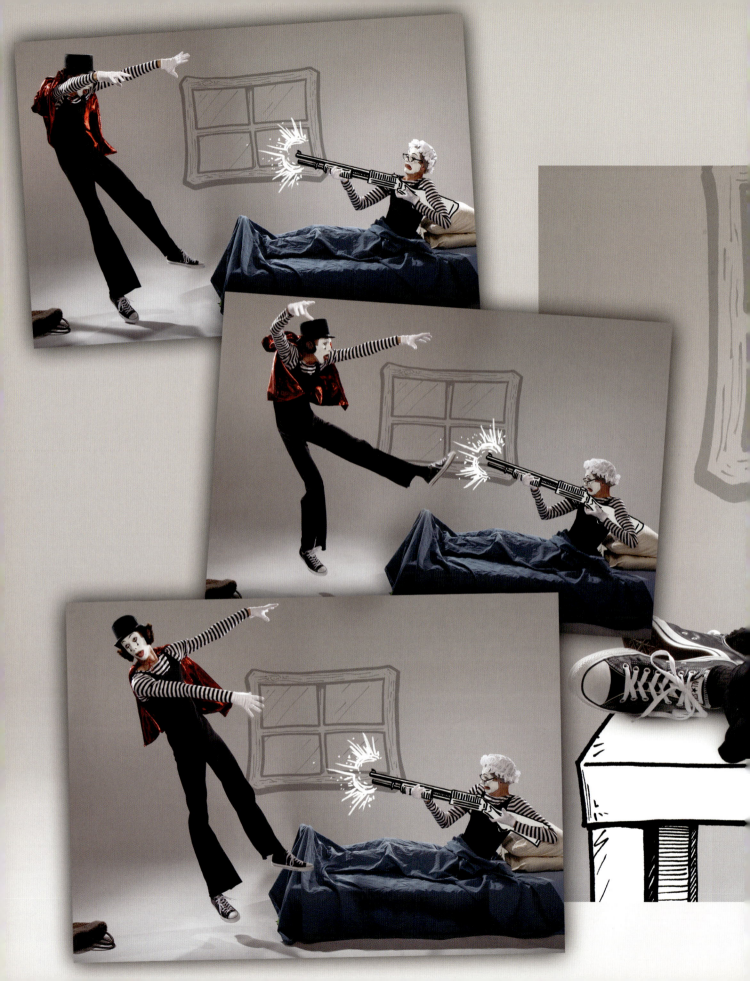

The Boy Who Mimed Wolf

L'imagerie différentes de mimes

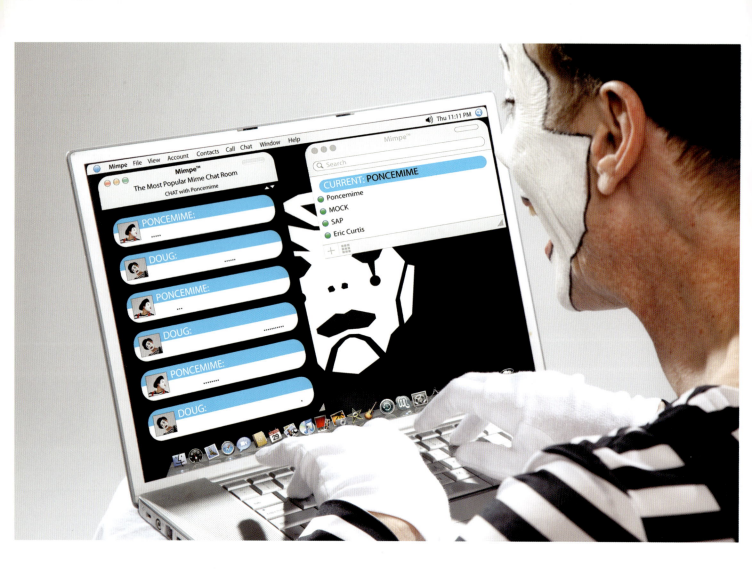

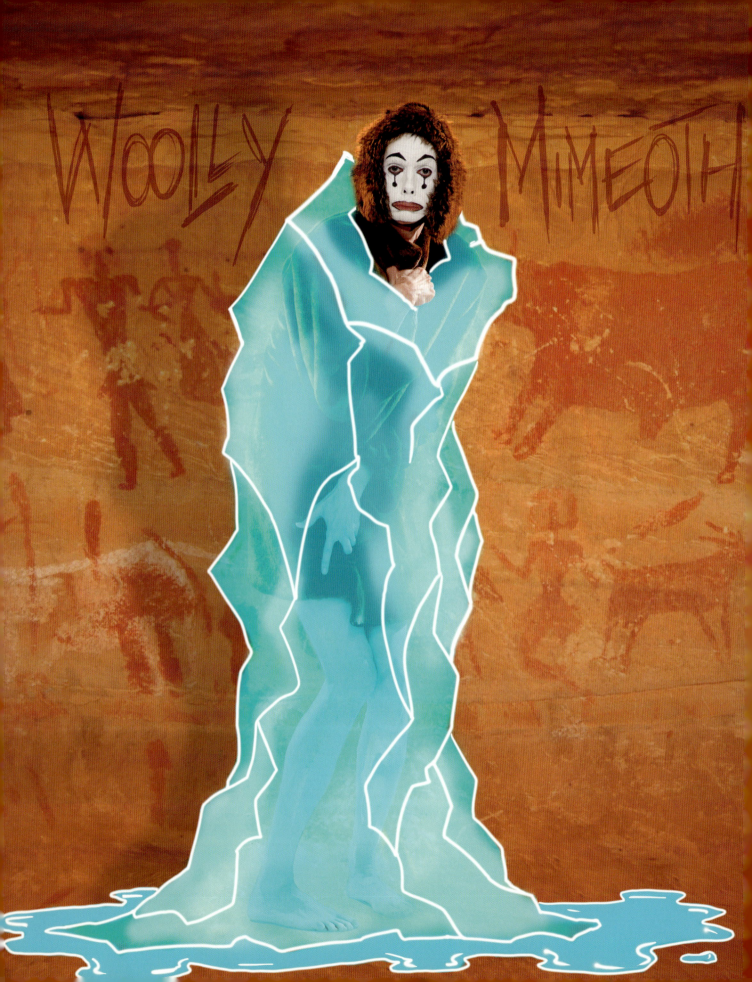

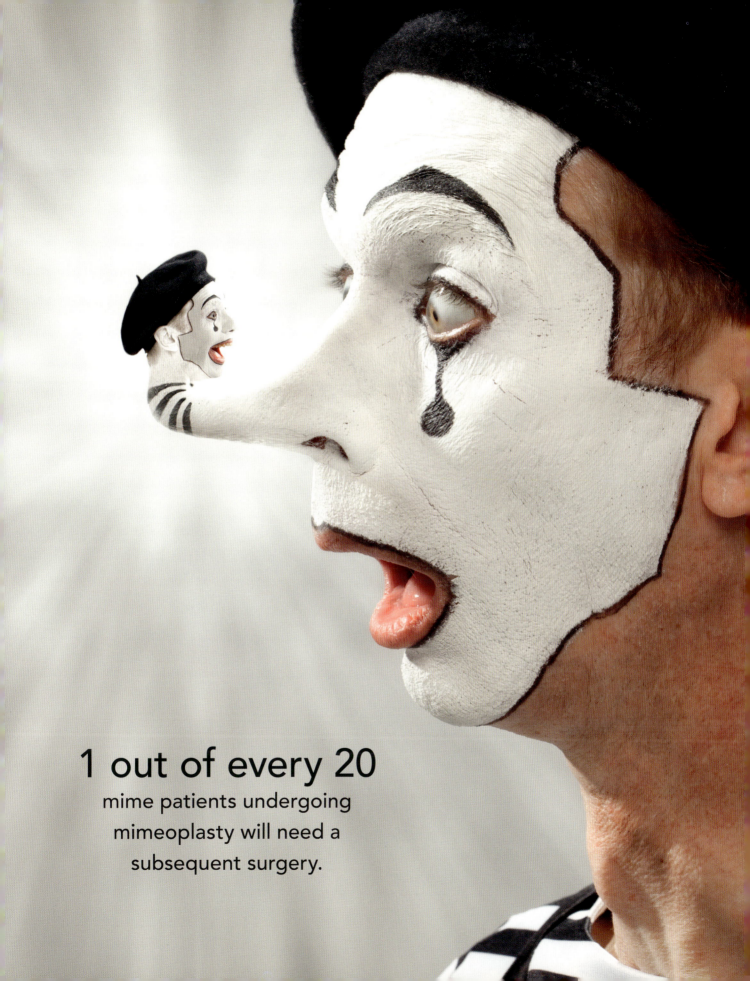

1 out of every 20

mime patients undergoing
mimeoplasty will need a
subsequent surgery.

HELP, mime fallen . . .

PACIFIC MIME   MOUNTAIN MIME

CENTRAL STANDARD MIME   EASTERN MIME

60%
of the time
MIMES
get infected
100%
of the time.

NO
GLOVE
NO
LOVE

CMC

ONE-TRACK MIME

You know what he's thinking about.

MIME OUT!

E 3   Treasurer of the State of Mime.   SERIES 2003   E 14

100   JONES   ONE H

FEDERAL RESERVE NOTE

PC18675309JM

D2

UNITED STATES
FEDERAL RESERVE SYSTEM

THIS NOTE IS VERY TENDER
FOR ALL MIMES, PUBLIC AND PRIVATE

Doug Jones

E 3   Treasurer of the State of Mime.   SERIES 2003   E 14

100   JONES   ONE H

FEDERAL RESERVE NOTE

PC18675310JM

D2

UNITED STATES
FEDERAL RESERVE

A MIMEOGRAM COULD SAVE YOUR LIFE.

THE MORE YOU KNOW

Mime in any language says love.

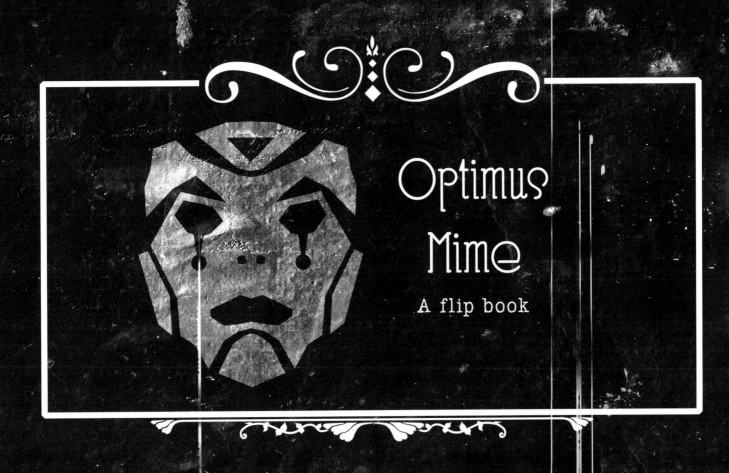

Optimus Mime

A flip book

Decisions
Decisions

MIME OF THE YEAR

MIME

Friends don't let friends mime drunk.

you drink, you mime, you lose.

We never talk anymore . . .

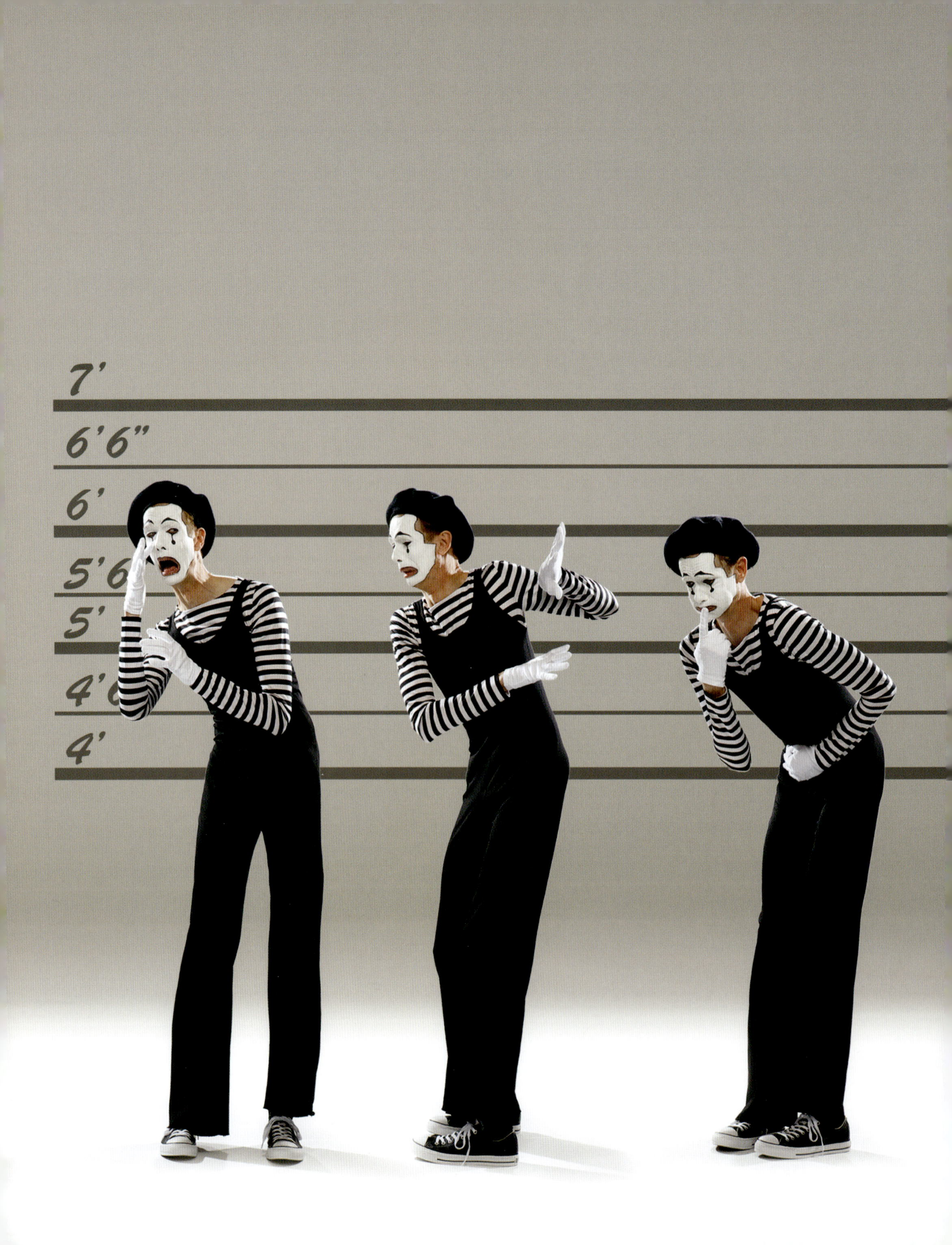
7'
6'6"
6'
5'6
5'
4'6
4'

Mimejitsu

The art of being seen and not heard

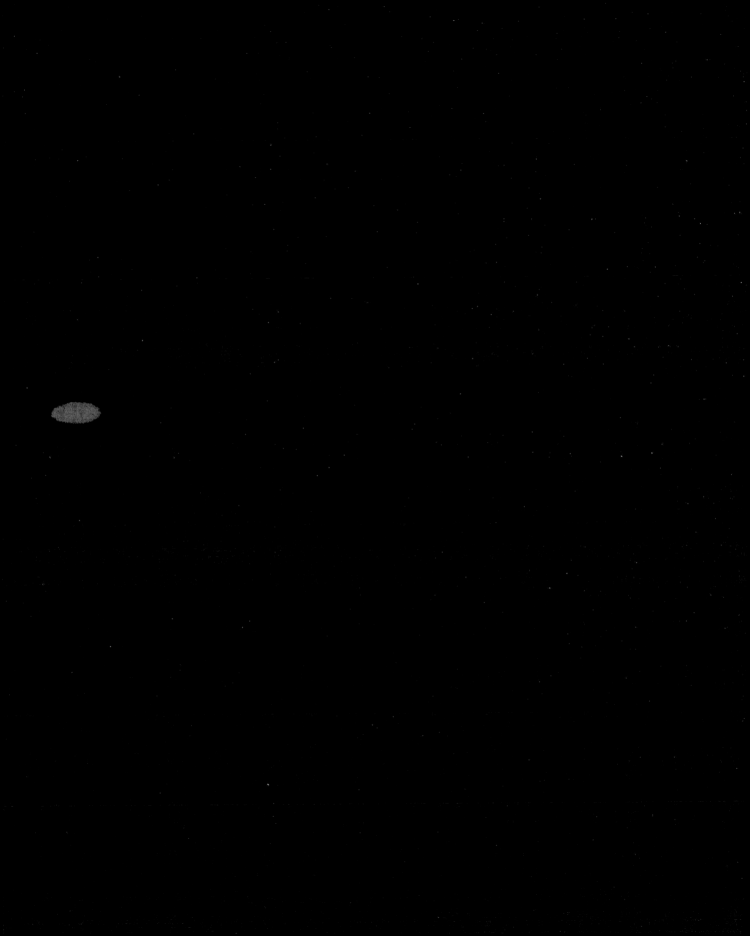

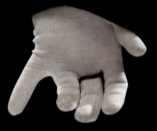

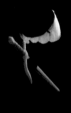

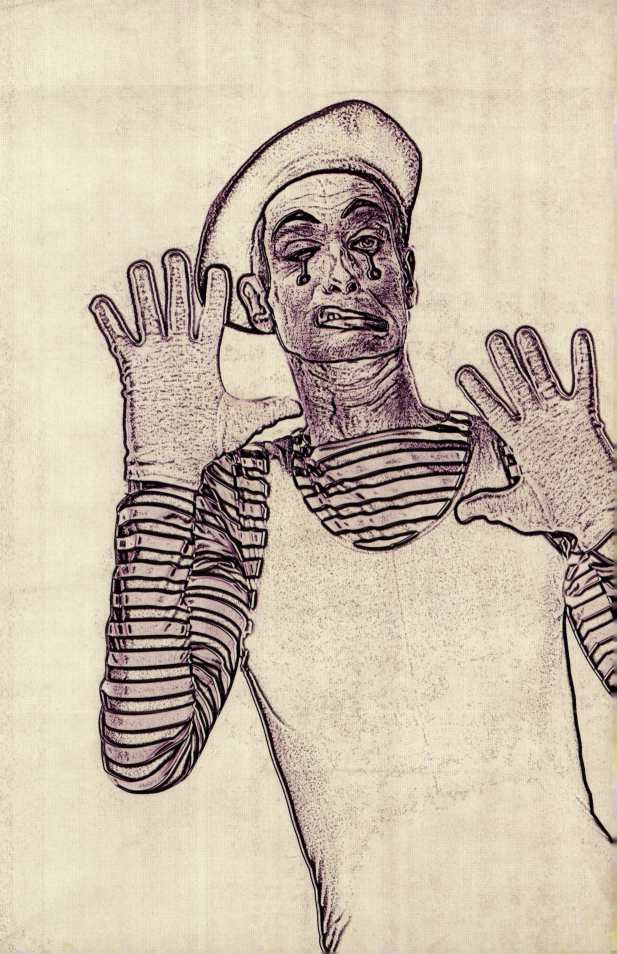

mimes of the round table

One small step for mime . . .

fin

ACKNOWLEDGMENTS

I need to thank the brilliant Adam Mock for sparking this idea in a hotel ballroom and for bringing together the genius wit of my longtime friend Scott Perry and the expert eye of Eric Curtis to make this silly dream of a book come true. To Helen Rosburg and the entire Medallion team: thank you for having such blind, er, deaf faith in us! Collaborating with you all has been a benchmark in my life. To Joshy Ponceman Perry: being in a lens with you always makes me happy. To my award-winning makeup artist, Thom Floutz, for slumming with us. To my lovely Mrs. Laurie for understanding when I don't want to *talk* and without whom I wouldn't be me. To my dear mother, Fifi, and father, Wawa, for teaching me that children should be *seen and not heard*. To my brothers, Bobby, Tommy, and Richie, for telling me to shut up—it finally paid off. To all my puppies for being the kids I never had. To Bob Rieth for being a father after my own passed. To Guillermo del Toro for turning this pathetic mime into a movie star. To manager Bruce Smith, appearance manager Derek Maki, publicists John Zander and Jess Knox, lawyer Philip Rosen, and first agent Philip Karr: you complete me. To webmaster Helen Chavez for propping me up with bosies. To all the Fan Sapiens: I wouldn't have a career without you. To anyone who ever hired me as a mime: you kept a starving young actor from actually starving. And finally to Reed K. Steele for his mentorship, teaching me the art of mime starting back in 1978, and for being the role model a skinny kid needed to dream big.

—Doug

Special thanks to PBS in the '70s for introducing me to *Monty Python*. To Dr. Harvey Bollich for his readings from *The Far Side* that began every day of my high school senior year. To the Jews—you meshuganas know how to make with the funny. To the Brits for being so socially repressed it's hilarious. To Jonathan Wenstrup, the best guy to food safari with while making filmed fun. To my Stah for always quelling my panics and being the best stah in the whole world. To my folks—you hepcats let me be me and that's rad-groovy. To Mema, who helped twist my brain in a very wonderful way. And to Mya and Kaylyn for letting me twist your brains. And of course, my bro, Josh "The Ponceman" Perry, for constantly throwing me mental curveballs that nail me in the ha-ha zone. I am uber-thankful to have found so many uber-talented mofos to make uber-cool art with. Uber.

—SAP

So grateful for Helen A Rosburg, who has always believed in me and in the vision for this book. Your friendship and support will always mean more than I can express. A huge thanks to my brilliant cocreators, SAP, Curtis, and Dougie. You took a seed of an idea and grew a forest. And to Ponce for simply being his wonderful self. James, Turo, and Michal, thank you for making this book look as sexy as a full-bodied wine, poignant yet not overbearing. And to every mime who ever was and who ever will be: your silent plight for equality is now heard within these pages. It's my hope that one day you'll be able to vote.

—Adam

To my high school photo teacher, Walt Pinto, the hippest hippie who started this gangsta sh@#!!! and busted out Dr. Dre's *The Chronic* in photo lab—that G always kep' it real. Huddy and Sofia, the god-brats, you kids keep me in check. To all my mime book homies and coconspirators: thanks for invading my home studio and ruining my sleep for three days. And to all those graphic fools at Medallion: you cats keep it gangsta. And Mark Ryden is da bomb. PEACE!

—Eric

ERIC CURTIS Presents

FALLEN SUPERHEROES

Photography and concept by Eric Curtis
Written by Scott Allen Perry & Adam Mock

Fallen Superheroes is a caricatured look at extraordinary everyday people through the visionary lens of professional photographer Eric Curtis. Using superheroes as the allegory, Curtis explores the not-so-glamorous and sometimes dark realities of those who strive to live their dreams against all odds. Curtis once again pairs his trademark imagery with the witty prose of Scott Allen Perry and Adam Mock, making *Fallen Superheroes* an eye-popping, gut-busting, esoteric commentary on the unique individuals who color our lives.

ISBN# 978-1605422-70-1
Trade Paperback / Coffee Table Book
US/CDN $24.95 / JUNE 2012

Mime Very Own Social Network

For cool shizz:

facebook.com/MimeMob

Follow the mime mob on

mimeveryownbook.com

@mimemob
twellow.com/Mimemob

Be in the know on the latest Medallion Press news by becoming a Medallion Press Insider!

As an Insider you'll receive:

· Our FREE expanded monthly newsletter, giving you more insight into Medallion Press

· Advanced press releases and breaking news

· Greater access to all your favorite Medallion authors

Joining is easy. Just visit our website at
www.medallionpress.com and click on
Super Cool E-blast next to the social media buttons.

Want to know what's going on with your favorite author or
what new releases are coming from Medallion Press?

Now you can receive breaking news, updates, and more from
Medallion Press straight to your cell phone, e-mail, instant messenger, or Facebook!

Sign up now at www.twitter.com/MedallionPress to stay on top of all the happenings in and around Medallion Press.

MEDALLION
P R E S S

medallionpress.com